COULD I SIT ON A CLOUD?

And Other Questions About Science

Kay Barnham

Raintree

Raintree is an imprint of Capstone Global Library Limited, a company incorporated in England and Wales having its registered office at 7 Pilgrim Street, London, EC4V 6LB – Registered company number: 6695582

www.raintreepublishers.co.uk
myorders@raintreepublishers.co.uk

Text © Capstone Global Library Limited 2014
First published in hardback in 2014
Paperback edition first published in 2015
The moral rights of the proprietor have been asserted.

Edited by Dan Nunn, Rebecca Rissman, and John-Paul Wilkins
Designed by Steve Mead
Picture research by Mica Brancic
Production by Sophia Argyris
Originated by Capstone Global Library Ltd
Printed and bound in China by CTPS

ISBN 978 1 406 25948 3 (hardback)
17 16 15 14 13
10 9 8 7 6 5 4 3 2 1

ISBN 978 1 406 25954 4 (paperback)
18 17 16 15 14
10 9 8 7 6 5 4 3 2 1

British Library Cataloguing in Publication Data
Barnham, Kay.
Could I sit on a cloud? and other questions about science. -- (Questions you never thought you'd ask)
502-dc23
A full catalogue record for this book is available from the British Library.

Acknowledgements
We would like to thank the following for permission to reproduce photographs: Getty Images pp. 15 (Paul Burns), 19 (Trujillo-Paumier); NASA p. 7; Science Photo Library p. 23 (David Parker); Shutterstock pp. 4 cloud (© Panom), 4 girl (© Photosindiacom, LLC), 5 (© Daniel Prudek), 6 moon (© godrick), 6 house (© nikkytok), 8 cornflower field (© Elenamiv), 8 picnic (© wavebreakmedia), 9 New York (© upthebanner), 9 London (© Bikeworldtravel), 9 Sydney (© Paul Coartney), 9 clock (© Rtimages), 10 (© Bertl123), 11 (© Jacqueline Watson), 12 (© Julien Tromeur), 13 (© Albert Barr), 14 cloud (© Panom), 14 boy (© WAMVD), 16 (© benicce), 17 (© Isantilli), 18 balloon (© Marynchenko Oleksandr), 18 drink can (© foodonwhite), 20 pavement (© Boobl), 20 stalk leg (© Ilya Akinshin), 21 (© ilolab), 22 girl (© Gelpi), 22 rainbow (© irin-k), 24 boy (© Anastasia Sukhonosova), 24 lightning (© prudkov), 25 (© Anton Petrus), 26 left man (© Monkey Business Images), 26 right man (© Jaimie Duplass), 26 Earth spinning (© charles taylor), 27 (© Aspen Photo), 28 Moon (© godrick), 28 sky (© mexrix), 28 girl (© First Class Photos PTY LTD), 29 (© gallofoto).

Cover photograph of cloud (© Panom) and smiling girl (© Photosindiacom, LLC) reproduced with permission of Shutterstock.

We would like to thank Diana Bentley and Marla Conn for their invaluable help in the preparation of this book.

Every effort has been made to contact copyright holders of any material reproduced in this book. Any omissions will be rectified in subsequent printings if notice is given to the publisher.

Disclaimer
All the internet addresses (URLs) given in this book were valid at the time of going to press. However, due to the dynamic nature of the internet, some addresses may have changed, or sites may have changed or ceased to exist since publication. While the author and publisher regret any inconvenience this may cause readers, no responsibility for any such changes can be accepted by either the author or the publisher.

CONTENTS

Some words are shown in bold, **like this**. You can find
out what they mean by looking in the glossary.

COULD I SIT ON A CLOUD?

No – you'd fall right through! Clouds might look **solid** but they are actually made of tiny **droplets** of water. These droplets are so light that they float in the air. Sometimes, the droplets join together to make bigger drops. When these drops become too heavy to float, they fall as rain, sleet, or snow.

If clouds were solid, mountains could not poke through them!

COULD ANYONE LIVE ON THE MOON?

In the 1960s and 1970s, astronauts travelled to the Moon. They stayed for about a day, but it would be tricky to live there for a long time. There's no air to breathe, no food to eat, and nowhere to live. But, if people could take enough of these things to the Moon with them, it might happen one day...

Did you know?

Earth's **atmosphere** protects us from the Sun's rays and gives us air to breathe. There is hardly any atmosphere on the Moon, so astronauts have to wear spacesuits for protection and to provide them with air.

IS IT THE SAME TIME ALL OVER THE WORLD?

No. When the Sun is highest in the sky, it is about midday. But because Earth is always spinning, midday happens at different times in different places. When it's breakfast time in the United States, it's lunchtime in Europe.

If we didn't have different **time zones**, some people might have to eat their lunch in the middle of the night!

WHY DON'T I FALL OUT OF A ROLLER COASTER WHEN IT GOES UPSIDE DOWN?

When you are moving, your body wants to keep travelling in a straight line. But as a roller coaster enters a loop-the-loop, the track goes upwards. As your body can't go forward any more, you get pushed into your seat instead. As long as the force pushing you into your seat is greater than the force of **gravity**, you won't fall out!

Did you know?

Roller coasters speed up as they plunge down huge slopes. This extra speed keeps the carriages going all the way round loops like this one.

WILL I EVER MEET AN ALIEN?

The truth is that no one knows. We might be alone in the universe. We might not. But there are many other stars that can support life, like the Sun supports life on Earth. There might be other planets like Earth going round these stars. So it's possible there could be aliens living on some of them…

Did you know?

There are hundreds of billions of stars in our **galaxy** and millions more galaxies beyond. So there are a LOT of stars out there!

CAN I MAKE MY OWN CLOUDS?

Sort of! Your breath contains **water vapour**, but you don't usually see it. However, when you breathe out on a cold day, the water vapour meets cold air, cools, and turns into water **droplets**. A single water droplet is too small to see, but when there are lots of them together, they look like clouds.

Just like your breath on a cold day, the clouds in the sky (see pages 4 and 5) are also formed from water droplets.

WHY DOES MY ICE CREAM DRIP DOWN MY ARM?

It's all because of **temperature**. When water freezes, it becomes ice, which is **solid**. When it warms, it becomes **liquid**. Ice cream contains water, so it stays solid in the freezer. But when you lick it on a sunny day, ice cream melts to become liquid.

Did you know?

You can make your own ice cream by mixing cream, sugar, and egg together and then freezing it. Create your own flavours by adding mashed up fruit.

HOW DOES THE FIZZ GET INTO FIZZY DRINKS?

Fizzy drinks have a **gas** called carbon dioxide forced into them. Then they are put into cans or bottles and the gas is trapped inside. When the drink is opened, bubbles of carbon dioxide escape from the **liquid**. This gives the drink its fizz!

WARNING: do not shake a fizzy drink. If you do, carbon dioxide above the liquid will be **reabsorbed** into the drink, making it so fizzy it explodes!

WHY AREN'T BIRDS ELECTROCUTED WHEN THEY SIT ON WIRES?

Electricity always travels down to the ground if it can. Birds stay safe because their legs only touch the power line. If birds had legs so long that one foot touched the ground as well, then electricity would be able to travel along their leg and down to the ground – and the bird would get frazzled!

BZZZT!

BZZZT!

CAN I MAKE MY OWN RAINBOW?

Sort of! Light is made up of all the colours we see in a rainbow. When sunlight shines through raindrops, the different colours form a rainbow in the sky. You can create a similar effect by shining a light through a **prism**. This lets you see the rainbow colours in light.

A prism is a specially shaped piece of glass or clear plastic.

DOES THUNDER EVER HAPPEN BEFORE LIGHTNING?

No, thunder always comes after lightning. Lightning happens when electricity jumps from cloud to cloud, or from a cloud down to the ground. Thunder is the sound that lightning makes. But because the speed of light is much faster than the speed of sound, we always see lightning before we hear it.

Did you know?

Light travels at 299,792,458 metres per second. But sound only travels through air at 343.2 metres per second.

IF EARTH IS SPINNING, WHY DON'T I FLY OFF INTO SPACE?

It is a force called **gravity** that stops you from taking off! Everything in the universe has gravity, but the bigger the object, the more gravity it has. Earth is very big indeed, so it has a lot of gravity and pulls you towards it.

However high we jump into the air, gravity always pulls us back down again with a bump!

WHY CAN I SEE THE MOON IN THE DAYTIME?

The Moon **orbits** Earth all the time, not just at night. So when the Moon is on our side of Earth in the daytime, we can sometimes see it. Stars shine during the day, too, but their light is much dimmer than sunlight, so we don't see them.

Did you know?
The Moon does not shine. Moonlight is actually light **reflected** from the Sun.

GLOSSARY

atmosphere layer of gases around a planet

droplet very small amount of liquid

galaxy collection of stars and other matter held together by gravity

gas substance, such as air, that can move around freely

gravity force that pulls everything towards Earth

liquid runny substance, such as water

orbit go round and round something

prism solid shape with no curves, often with triangular ends

reabsorb take in or soak up something again

reflect bounce back, usually light

solid hard or firm

temperature how hot or cold something is

time zone area on our planet where all the clocks are set to the same time

water vapour very tiny droplets of water

FIND OUT MORE

Books

First Encyclopedia of Science (Usborne, 2011)

Science Experiments, Robert Winston (Dorling Kindersley, 2011)

Space (Up Close), Paul Harrison (Franklin Watts, 2010)

Websites

www.kidsastronomy.com
Discover all there is to know about the solar system and space exploration on this website.

www.sciencemuseum.org.uk
Find out about science on the Science Museum's website. You could even visit the museum to learn more.

INDEX